# Healing

## Is for

# ALL

# Healing Is for ALL

A collection of poetry, marking the path
to healing the heart

Patricia Marquez-Singh

Artwork by Kat Farley

The only moment is the present moment.
In this moment, everything is perfect.
The real gift is the present.

# Contents

# Why I Wrote This Book

We are all healing from something. Sometimes we don't even recognize that we are or that we need to. But the heart does and when we fully know that truth, we can begin a new life.

I know I have needed healing many times throughout my life. Healing is a part of me and my journey in life. Even at a young age, as I saw the dark side of humanity, I also experienced the goodness in people. I witnessed genuine compassion, moments of pure joy, and acts of true faith and courage all around me. The feelings and emotions evoked by those experiences stayed with me and began to create a poetic rhythm in my heart.

Here, every poem is a testament to those feelings and emotions, every reflection is a unique experience. And together they tell a story

They tell the story of my own healing journey, one that is far from over.

May these words help you find peace, comfort and, most of all, healing. May it remind you that you are enough and exactly where you are supposed to be. May they serve as a reminder that you are worthy—worthy of healing.

My greatest hope is that my healing journey will invite you into your own journey and that we may find each other along the way.

I see you, I hear you.

# healing words

*Healing is the first step to any path.*

Healing is both a tool and an experience that allows us to see one another as equally human. It allows us to reconnect with ourselves and acknowledge our own humanity. To heal is to know one's self so we may move about the world and know one another. Healing helps us to build the courage necessary to do all of this.

Healing is an inside job

It is a deeply personal journey, unique to every person

It is not linear

It is not about getting from point A to point
B, it is about all the moments in between

You can be healing and hurting at the same time

Healing is messy

It has very little to do with anything or anyone else

Healing requires that we confront what gets in the way

The healing process begins when we tell the truth,
the truth about who and what we've been being

So that we can be who we are meant to be.

# Healing is for ALL

They say healing is for "those" people.

They say healing is for the suffering, the
people too afraid to be themselves.

They say healing is for the lost and not found.

They say healing is for the poor and hungry.

They say healing is for the people in pain,
the ones that "feel too much".

They say healing is for the disconnected and disillusioned.

They say healing is for those that are hurting.

They say healing is for those that are isolated and alone.

"They" ARE "those" people.

"We" are "those" people, so you see,
I am you and you are me.

Healing is for ALL.

Ingredients
for
healing)

# Part 1:

# purpose

We make an impact in the world just by expressing ourselves and being our true authentic selves.

Thank you for the difference you make in this world.

# I Am

"Who am I?" you ask
Well, I am many things

I am a
Mother, Wife, Daughter, Sister, Aunt, Cousin,
Friend, Godmother, Niece, Granddaughter

I am a
Teacher, Student, Disruptor, Guide, Dreamer,
Storyteller, Healer, Facilitator, Coach, Advocate

I am a
Child of God, Bridge Builder, Change Agent,
Community Partner, Circle Keeper, Truth Seeker,
Motivational Speaker, Holistic Educator

Some days I don't know who I am yet
I am many things yet to become

*And many things to unbecome so I can*

*become who I am meant to be*

*So, ask me tomorrow and I might be a different person*

*We always are*

# A Rumble

I turn on my T.V.

And all I hear are rough words

Hate, Prejudice, Ignorance

It describes itself with a crash,
clank, bang, and thunder

I turn on my T.V.

And all I hear are people shouting

It sounds like spike, slap, scratch, and crack

And it's not really worth it

Because in the end it's all a rumble

# The Transformation of Fear

Having courage doesn't mean you're not afraid

I have often found that in my most courageous
moments I also experienced deep fear

It means you master it, you face it, you transform it

You no longer let it stand in the way of following your
life's purpose or doing what is right and just

Fear has no power as soon as it transforms

All things worth doing, all dreams worth
pursuing often come with fear

It is the price we pay for greatness

Our job is to recognize it, accept it and then just be great.

# It Keeps Me

Keep laughing

Keep questioning

Keep judging

Keep doubting

Keep conspiring

It keeps me

It keeps me going

It adds fuel to my fire so that it may keep shining

My only question is:

Is all that laughing and questioning and judging
and doubting and conspiring keeping you?

Keeping you prisoner of your own shame, your
own insecurities, your own judgement, your
own doubt, and your own self-sabotage?

# The Great Paradox

Being comfortably uncomfortable is the new normal

We have to get comfortable with being
afraid and making mistakes

We have to get comfortable with just being ourselves

We have to get comfortable with speaking our truth

It is all part of life

It is all part of the journey

And it is where growth and progress live

# Sleepy Transformation

I wish to be like a Monarch Butterfly

Epitome of transformation

Known as a wanderer, iconic

Famous for seasonal migration and natural metamorphosis

"Sleepy Transformation"

More than beautiful, they contribute
to the health of our planet

A symbol of healing and hope

# Dreams Worth Pursuing

I always thought my dreams were
unattainable, beyond my reach

"You can't do that", they said

"You're crazy", they said

"You're not smart enough", they said

"You're not brave enough", they said

"You are not worthy", they said

"Your dreams are too big", they said

Until I realized my dreams were not big
enough, they were not scary enough

Those were the dreams worth fighting for

Those were the dreams worth the courage to
defend and protect what I most desired

These are the dreams worth pursuing

These are my dreams and I am worthy

# A Yearning...

That yearning you feel, it is there for a reason

Follow it wherever it may lead for it may lead to greatness

It may lead you into the truth of your dreams

That yearning is your calling, it is your gift to the world

Follow it

Follow it through treacherous paths,
paths that seem to be confused

Follow it up steep hills and the tallest mountains

And despite your tiredness and slow
pace there is progress to be made

There is growth to be discovered

There are dreams to be made reality*

That yearning is the gentle tug
that God has placed in your heart to
return you to who you really are

It is a constant reminder that there is more
to be done, that there is more to dream

Follow it, that yearning

It knows the way

The world is waiting...

# O What a Task

To elevate humankind
To inspire love and courage
To share compassion and grace
To support creativity and dreams
To encourage peace and transformation
To seek understanding and truth
To cultivate human connection
To advocate for justice and social change
To celebrate successes and failures, big and small
To spread joy and kindness
O what a task
O what beauty
O what a privilege

# Therefore I Am

I have been called
A Peacemaker
A Thought Partner
A Defender
A Poet
An Upstander
A Lightworker
A Rock
A Steady Force
A Listener
An Advisor
A Lawyer
A Mediator
A Mentor
A Counselor
A Champion
To be that which I am called
Who am I not to be?

# The Fight, The Legacy

This fight is nothing new

We have been here before

The relentless pursuit for social justice, equity,
human resistance, compassion, human dignity

The legacy is very much alive

We continue the fight

What is also very much alive is the courage, the
hope, and the compassion of the human spirit

The presence of hope when things don't
seem or feel hopeful is alive in all of us

Let us move forward guided by the values of
determination, resiliency, dignity, and compassion

In service to the legacy left behind by
those who fought before us

May these words serve as a reminder that none of us
have to wait to create change, none of us have to wait
to serve, none of us have to wait to show compassion

Within all of us is the power to inspire and empower

And a reminder that none of us have to
do it alone, we are all connected

In this together

This fight, our fight

"Let us find our ground
so we may stand upon it
with pride and dignity."

Ingredients for healing)

# Part 2: Faith

"I cannot see it, but I can feel it, and that is enough."

# The Leap

Taking the biggest leap of faith

Realizing the dream my ancestors had for me

The dream that belongs to us

It is terrifying and beautiful at the same time

Dreams worth pursuing usually are

The leap is much less scary because I know they
are behind me and in front of me, leading the way

# Duality

As we navigate these crucial times

We are reminded that while there is
uncertainty and rough roads ahead

There is a duality that exists

Where there is Darkness there is Light

Where there is Fear there is Courage

Where there is Sadness there is Happiness

Where there is Doubt there is Hope

Where there is Pain there is Healing

Where there is Grief there is Life

But these are not opposites—no

They are one

It is a matter of which you believe in,
which you choose to see

# Darkness Is Not

Darkness is not the absence of light

Darkness is where light lives
just waiting to shine brightly
onto its believer

Where there is darkness
there is light waiting
to shine, waiting to
be released

Waiting for you to
see it, waiting for you
to believe in the light there
is within and around you

No matter how dark the day
seems or how dark your heart
feels, light is still there, seeking
entrance, waiting for you to notice.

Do you see it? Do you feel it?

The light is you...

# Fear Not

I am grateful for my fear

It grounds me and humbles me

Through my fear I know the ground I stand on

Through my fear I know my limitations

Through my fear I know how small and
great I am at the same time

Through my fear I can transform

Myself and the world

It is through my fear that I learn to rely
on something greater than myself

Therefore, I fear not

# Love Masked in Sadness

Once we experience grief it never leaves us, it changes

It hits us all of a sudden with an impact
so rapid and profound

But doesn't leave as quickly

It hits us slow, with a gentle pull and leaves
us before we can shed the first tear

It shows up like the waves, some crashing and
overwhelming its witness, some softly caressing wet skin

And once it's passed through all of its
changes, it transforms into Love again

For grief is just love masked in sadness

Grief is all of those things

# The Greatest Reminder

Every moment of anxiety, grief,
fear is an invitation

An invitation to breathe

To harness the power of being still and allowing
God to work on our behalf, to carry us, to
guide us and to remind us that we are far
stronger, wiser, and resilient than we think

# Your Future Self Will Thank You

One day you will look back and think
about this dark time as a blessing

As an opportunity to learn, to grow,
to appreciate all you do have

To see the light there still is

To trust

To have faith in what you cannot see

To have faith in yourself

Keep going, keep moving, keep fighting

Everything will be so good so soon

# Memories

I remember it like it was yesterday

It took our breath away

Time stood still

The final goodbye was endless

I tried to live without feeling

It didn't work

Life doesn't work that way

I learned the hard way

Who would have known

We were never the same

You and I
Nor should we be
Nor would we want to be
You
I
A whisper in the wind
A shadow in the dark
A fleeting gaze in the crowd
We never were
But a memory

# Grief Is My Friend

I met grief a long time ago and it has never left me

Sometimes it leaves for a period of time but then
returns to remind me I have loved hard

It reminds me I have loved with every inch of my being

It reminds me that we grieve hard because we Love hard

It reminds me of the life I once had and
how wonderful my new life is

It reminds me of all the people I cannot see anymore
but live in me and shape the way I live my life, for I
want to be all of the things I loved about the people
who are no longer here in this physical world

I want to be wise, bold, kind, funny,
strong, fearless, courageous

My friend Grief reminds me of that

# The Nature of Existence

The presence of absence

How can something that is absent be so present?

It's absent because it is not here

But I feel it, I feel its presence

Its existence is real, yet it doesn't exist here and now

It is somewhere and everywhere and nowhere

# Peace

Peace does not mean to be in the absence
of noise, stress, chaos, anxiety

Peace does not mean there aren't
things happening around you

Peace doesn't depend on the outside world

Peace has to grow from within, it lives in you

Peace is cultivated through proactive action

Peace is a state of mind

# Heart Work

This work is hard. Heart work usually is

It is about digging deep even when we
are afraid of what we will find

It is about confronting what gets in the way
even when the answer is ourselves

It is about telling the truth no matter where it leads

This requires vulnerability, courage, and trust

And a willingness to receive and to give

In return we are rewarded in ways we could never imagine

Liberation

Joy

Healing

Transformation

I say that's worth it

# Gifts to Come

Don't be ashamed of your neediness

It heightens your awareness

And sometimes we are forced into awareness

An awareness we were not prepared for or even wanted

Being keenly aware of your neediness
is not a weakness or a lack

It is an opportunity to practice gratitude, patience and faith

An opportunity to prepare for the gifts to come

Don't be ashamed of your emptiness

What a blessing it is to know you have space to be filled

To know your heart longs for connection

As you become fully aware

That neediness and that emptiness are transformed

Transformed into abundance

Abundance of joy and beauty and love and Life

All you have to do is ready the way

Are you willing to receive all that is to come?

"The answers are always there. We just have to slow down enough to see them."

Ingredients for healing

Part 3:

Compassion

You are worthy of all
things beautiful.

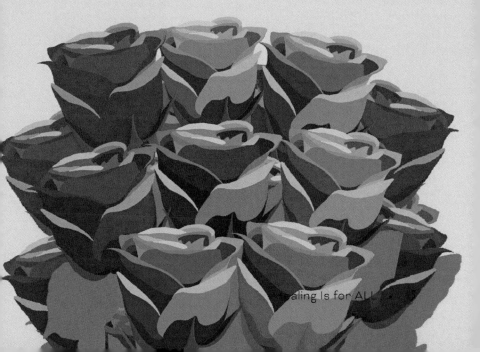

# Beauty

Beauty isn't made, it isn't caused—IT Simply IS

IT IS:

The Sun

The Tree

The Monarch Butterfly

A flower

The body and soul of a Mother who has just given birth

Her body that says, "I just spent months building
and creating a person inside me and now my
body is a reflection of my strength, my resiliency,
my unwavering love and my wisdom"

A sunset

My wrinkles and gray hair

The Earth as it adapts to the conditions
of time, season after season...

It is... You... just as you are...

# Beauty, Magic, Courage

Not the sky not the sun nor the stars or the moon or
the oceans or the rarest flower or tallest mountain

Can compare to the beauty that is you

Not the galaxy not the universe nor all
of space or the fastest rocket

Can compare to the magic that is you

Not the bravest warrior not the strongest soldier nor
all the armies or the fastest fighter or boldest voice

Can compare to the courage that is you

# Love Letter

I love you for who you are

Not for what you do or what you have

I don't love you despite your
imperfections and flaws

I love you because of them

I love you because you choose
your imperfections

You recognize them, you
embrace them

You are not perfect, and you
are not afraid to admit it

I love you because you
know there is much
you don't yet
know about
the world

Always willing to grow, and
learn, and teach, and share

I love you because you don't
take yourself too seriously

Always open to humor, to smile,
and to laugh at yourself

I love you because you fail

Always celebrating the near win as a success

I love you because sometimes
you get it wrong

Always accepting it with grace and humility

I love you because you don't
have all the answers

Always willing to search, discover,
uncover, and ultimately
surrender if necessary

I love you because
even when your best
falls short

It is still the
best

# The Next Big Thing

Why are we always looking for the next BIG thing?

The next great idea

The next product that will make life
easier or make you look younger

The next inspiration that will change the world

You are looking in the wrong place

Instead of looking outward you need to look inward

YOU are the next BIG thing

YOU are the next great idea

YOU are the next inspiration

You are what the world is waiting for

Go for it...

BE who you were always meant to be...

The Next BIG Thing...

# *Love*

What if the answer is love?

An unconditional, unwavering, force field of love

The kind of love that doesn't depend on
what happens or doesn't happen

A kind of love that knows no bounds, or limits or boundaries

A kind of love that transcends time
and space and conditions

A kind of love that cannot be explained or described

A kind of love that can only be experienced

A kind of love that just IS

Love not so much as a feeling or sentiment but a commitment,
a call to action that all of our words and all of our actions will
come from a place of God

What if?

# " The Real Worry "

We often overestimate the likelihood
that something bad will happen

"If this doesn't get done then this will happen"

"If I don't do this then I will let someone down"

"If I say something, then someone will be angry,
disappointed, hurt...they won't like me"

But in all that worrying we forget who we are

Because more often than that we
underestimate our capacity to overcome our
obstacles, our challenges, our fears

The real worry should be

"Am I forgetting who I am and where I come from?"

"Am I betraying myself to make others comfortable?"

# One Day

Maybe one day I will finally believe in myself

Maybe one day I will decide to live by my
own expectations and guidelines

Maybe one day I will declare that I
have enough and I am enough

Maybe one day I will know love and be love

Maybe one day I will no longer be afraid

Maybe one day I will no longer doubt myself

Maybe one day I will actually feel
worthy of my own greatness

Maybe... that day... is... Today

# Forgiveness

"How can I forgive what I can't forget?" you ask
You don't
It is about remembering
It is about returning to your own sacredness
Forgiveness requires our cooperation
We forgive to free our soul

# Surrender

An act of courage and grace

A refinement of our movement in life

A choice to live

An opportunity to make space for what is truly valuable

To make space for what truly matters

To recognize that you can no longer
be trapped by the weight

You can no longer be held captive

Not weakness, not giving up, not admitting defeat

On the contrary

You win

Because you choose life

A life well lived

Greatest act of liberation

To acknowledge I can no longer carry this alone

I surrender to something greater than myself so that
I may walk in peace and beauty about the world

I surrender

# On Being Silent

We say so much in silence
When we are silent we say:
I see you
I hear you
I am with you
You are not alone
You are worthy
You matter

When I am silent it doesn't mean I
don't have anything to say

It means I am taking the time and space
I need to reflect and process

My silence doesn't mean I am absent,
it means I am present

It means I am choosing powerfully and
wisely to find words of love and compassion
and comfort and reassurance

It means I am giving you time to find your own silence

So, in a way... silent is the loudest thing you can be

# A Gentle Nudge

If I could take your sadness away I would

If I could take your anger away I would

If I could take your grief away I would

If I could take your hopelessness
away I would

If I could make all your pain go away I would

But I can't

Only you can do that

That sadness, that anger, that grief, that
hopelessness, that pain belongs to you

You need it to remind you of how strong you
are and how much stronger you will be when
you come out of it on the other side

And I will be right there waiting for you on the other side

And I am right here now with a gentle
nudge to help you on your way

# At the Speed of Trust

Trust happens when we feel Safe

We feel safe only when we are truly Seen and Heard

We all desire change in the world.

Positive, impactful change.

The thing about change is that it
happens at the speed of trust.

Trust in people, trust in processes and systems,
and most importantly trust in ourselves.

And the thing about trust is that we
can only trust if we feel safe.

But safety is only achieved when we
are truly seen and heard.

And so you see, in order for any change to occur
we must first acknowledge our own humanity.

# Heavy

Your words hurt me

But not as much as they hurt you

You must be so tired

Tired of carrying around all that pain,
all that shame, all that burden

It must be so heavy

Why do you hold on to it?

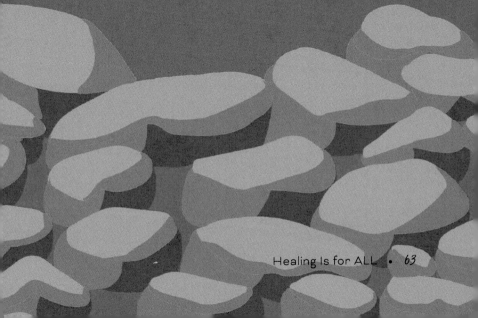

# The Only Way

I hope you are OK
I hope you feel the impact of that pain, that trauma
Yes, I hope you feel it
It is the only way
It is the only path to healing
You can't ignore it
You can't suppress it
You can't bury it
You can't deny it or pretend it doesn't exist
That will only breed more pain
You can't go over it or under it or around it

That may work for a while but eventually the pain will multiply and pour out of you as it screams to be released to be recognized

The only way is through it

That is where healing is, waiting for you

You will be OK

# Keep Moving

It is a moment in time

A brief snapshot in a complete life

Much more life to live

You are not stuck here

You are not broken

Nothing is broken

It can feel that way, yes

It is not a place to stay

Pay attention to when it's time to move again

You will know

If you want to know

It may be messy, it may be scary

But it should be

The movement is healing

Keep moving

This too shall pass

# Perfectly Imperfect

I am not perfect nor do I pretend to be

I am full of flaws, imperfections, mistakes

Some days I am a hot mess

Some days I struggle to find hope and love

Some days I feel lonely and disconnected

Most days I am optimistic and hopeful

Most days I am present and joyful

Most days I see light over darkness

I am full of love, beauty, wisdom, life

And some days I am all of these things all at once

I acknowledge it

I choose it

I embrace it

And once I do, I can move forward unburdened
by what was, what is and what will be

I am perfectly imperfect

# Imagine

Imagine a circle of compassion and
no one standing outside of it

I heard that once

Imagine if that could be

Imagine if no one ever felt alone or
abandoned or forgotten or ignored

Imagine

Imagine if every ounce of sadness or grief
or despair or hopelessness was met with
kindness and hope, and love and compassion

Imagine

Imagine compassion as an expression
that requires action

Imagine compassion as the antidote
for all that ails our heart

Imagine if that's all it took

Imagine

# With Broken Spirit

They tell you to fly and then
cut your wings off

They tell you to create and
then kill your spirit

They tell you to reach for the
stars and then drag you down

They tell you to dream and
then call you crazy

They tell you to be yourself but not too much

Why do they do that?

Perhaps because someone did it to them
and they didn't know how to transform
their pain, so instead they transferred it

What a true shame that is

# No One

I have often wondered why no one recognized your pain

Why no one noticed your loneliness

Why no one felt your suffering

But then I discovered they were trapped, paralyzed too

Paralyzed by their own fear

They had already learned to oppress their own feelings

They were suffering too

So how could they?

Save you

They needed saving too

I'm sorry I wasn't there, I couldn't be

And yet you are here

Despite so much—you are here

And I am here now

We are here now—together

# Whole

Replacing the idea of wellness
with wholeness

Focusing more on feeling whole, complete

Well-being is a personal journey

It is a relationship with one's self
to achieve wholeness based on
personal expectations and values

# A Healing Pause

I know you feel as if you must keep going

Even as you are depleted of energy,
time, sleep, resources, and joy

But that is not the way for you

You were meant to take a healing pause,
to take a step back from the mess

To take the time you need to reflect,
to breathe, and to just BE

And once you do you can keep moving
to the rhythm of your own life

A new life

"There is no real balance, only nimbleness."

Ingredients
for
healing

Part 4:

joy

Life is full of sweetness.
You just have to have a sweet tooth.

# A new life

A new way of being

A new way of moving in the world

A new way of showing up

A new experience we enter into

A choice

An action

A decision

Darkness does not live in this new life

Sorrow is but a memory

Doubt is no more

Fear does not thrive here

In this new life

# The Power of Perception

Your eyes are open, but you cannot see

I wish you could see yourself the way I see you

You see what you want to see

You have ears that hear but are not attuned

You hear what you want to hear

What do you want to see?

What do you want to hear?

# Less Is More

Simplicity doesn't mean smallness or insignificance

It doesn't mean it is not important or great or beautiful

It doesn't mean it has no value or quality

It means we are choosing a way of life that allows
us to appreciate the simpler, that allows us to
see the perfect in the imperfect, that allows
us to see the beauty among the chaos

Sometimes less is more

# In Your Presence

What a blessing it is to be in your presence

To experience your joy and wonder and compassion

To feel your love and energy and kindness for all

To have a sense of peace and calm and reassurance

Being in your presence is being enveloped
in the warmest of hugs

A hug that never leaves even when you do

Being in your presence is everything

What a true blessing

# Smile

When you smile, I smile
When you laugh, I laugh
When you dance, I dance
When you love, I love
When you frown, I frown
When you hurt, I hurt
When you cry, I cry
When you grieve, I grieve
And when you're ready...
We will smile again—together

# Sing

It is time to let your quiet soul sing

It is time to give your heart permission to sing its own song

It is time to prepare your body to feel
the rhythm of its own tune

It is time to create the beat of your own life

It is time to sing out loud

It is time to live your life out loud

# Dance

My heart is dancing

My heart is dancing because
you are here, not there, or
anywhere, but here, in my heart

My spirit is dancing

My spirit is dancing
because it is free

My soul is dancing

My soul is dancing because
it has known love

Our hearts dance
together because we
have each other

Dance my darling,
dance

# Silence

Even silence makes a sound

It sounds like hopelessness

It sounds like desperation

It sounds like loneliness

It sounds like sadness

It sounds like you are screaming at the top
of your lungs but no sound is heard

Silence is loud I've found

Silence is being surrounded by noise
but you can't hear a thing

Even silence makes a sound

# Wear Peace Like a Cloak

Stillness, quietness

That is where growth, peace, and healing live

It is where we learn to reconnect with each other

It is where we learn to reconnect with ourselves

It is where we can tap into our inner resources that support our collective and individual well-being

At first, we may need to make intentional time for stillness, for quietness

But eventually, we learn to wear it like a cloak

Always hanging loosely over you so that when you are in need of stillness and quietness it is there

We learn to carry it with us so that when we are in need of peace we can unpack it

# Take Flight

As the wind blows birds take flight

As if needing the extra push to send them on their way

As the rain falls the earth rejoices

As if needing a blanket of life

As the sun shines flowers bloom

As if needing permission to come out

And just like the birds and the earth and the flowers

You take flight

# Love, Part 2

Have you ever seen anything so beautiful?

Have you ever heard anything so pleasant?

Have you ever known a love like this?

Have you ever felt more alive?

No, this is the first time…

# Heartbeat

My heartbeat tells me when I feel loved

My heartbeat tells me when I feel joy

My heartbeat tells me when I feel connected

My heartbeat tells me when I am seen and heard

It slows down as I take in the beauty
and magic of the moment

And for just that moment time stands still

My heartbeat tells me when I am nervous

My heartbeat tells me when I am afraid

My heartbeat tells me when I feel
disconnected and disappointed

My heartbeat tells me when something is not right

My heartbeat tells me when I am on the
verge of a breakthrough or breakdown

It speeds up as it encourages me to speak
up, to fight back, to cry, to love again

Can you hear it, my heartbeat?

I can, it tells me much.

# Joy

A step beyond happiness

It is not a destination, it is not fleeting

Joy comes from within, it comes from the depths of your soul, your heart, your spirit

It is a constant inner state of being

Joy is the face of your child, their laughter, their wonderous spirit

Joy is the warmth you feel when you go home

Joy is living a life of purpose

Joy is a deep sense of belonging

Joy is having faith and hope and a knowing that you are never alone

Joy is unshakeable

*Abundance is not an amount of something.*
*It is an experience, a context we create for ourselves where we declare "I have enough" and "I am enough".*

Ingredients
for
healing

Part 5:
belonging

"The only thing we have to belong to is ourselves."

# She Belongs

She is blindsided
In this room
In the space she is taking up
Where she never thought she could
Where she never thought she had a place
In this room
Sit in it
This space
She belongs
She sits in it with confidence and grace
She is blindsided
In this room
By the depth and weight of her presence
By the light and life of her existence
In this room
Sit in it
This space
She belongs
She always did

# Knowing Her Worth

All of a sudden everything made sense

She no longer needed anyone's approval, permission,
or acceptance to be who she was always meant to be

To be who she had been being but didn't know it yet

All of a sudden it all clicked

She could no longer be afraid

She could no longer hide

She could no longer make herself small

She could no longer betray herself to make others
feel more comfortable, or better about themselves

All of a sudden she knew she was worthy of so much more

# Where You Are

You are exactly where you are supposed to be

I know it doesn't feel like it but you are

For even today before night falls you are among
the stars and the moon and the vast sky

And when the sun rises again you will be there next to
the glowing sun, bursting with warmth and light and life

# In This Place

I am not sure what this place is

But I've seen it before many times

I am not sure where this place is

But I've been there before many times

In this place joy is abundant

In this place the sun is always shining and even when it tries to rain, the sun always peaks its way through as if to say, "No, only sunshine here"

In this place love is endless, unconditional, transcendent and transparent

In this place no one is ever afraid, no one is ever sad

Because no one is ever alone

In this place there is nothing more important than the relationship we have with one another and with ourselves

That is where I want to be

So I will return to a place I've never been

If for only in my dreams...

# Home

"Welcome home", she said

And with those words, a lifetime of longing came flooding in

A longing to know who and what I am

To know where I came from and who I come from

With those words I knew and felt it all, I knew I was home

I come from a faraway place where the earth
is covered with the sweat, blood and tears
of the people who tend to the land

I come from a people of fierce warriors and
fighters and teachers and students who refuse
to give up, who refuse to be defined by the color
of their skin or the language of their tongue

I come from a place of abundant beauty and culture
and traditions and values and teachings and wisdom
and foods that fill your belly and your soul

I come from a proud people, passionate people, people full
of life, people who are not done fighting, people who will
always stand up for what they deserve and what they have

I am all of these things

This was the last time we were both home

This is Home, "Welcome home"

# This Circle

Look at the Circle!

It is Beautiful

In this Circle you are welcomed, you are embraced, you are seen, you are heard, you are sacred, you are loved

This circle is beautiful

It holds the whole world and only you all at the same time

It holds the medicine, healing, compassion, connection we all seek

This circle is beautiful because you are in it

This circle is beautiful and so are you

## Connection

The greatest threat to our extinction is

Lack of connection

Connection with each other and connection with ourselves

Human connection

We should be worried indeed

Without connection we are truly alone

# You Are Not Alone

As you navigate your existence in this world

Remember you are not alone in that journey

I am finding my way too

Let's navigate together and find each other
in the midst of all the noise and chaos

For together we belong in this world

Ingredients
for
healing

Part 6:
Family

Home is my Power.

# The Journey of Greatness

The greatness has traveled far and wide

It has traveled through many peaks and valleys

It has traveled by land, sea, and air

It has traveled through rain and shine

It has traveled through more generations
than I will ever fully know

My ancestors carried it, that greatness

Now it's mine

Mine to carry forward for the travel is not over

The journey of greatness continues

# Apa

Apa,

That is my grandfather

Strength

Resilient

Persevering

Sacrifice

Chasing trains for the chance to work

For the chance to eat

Humor

Encouragement

Love

Rides to school

All you gave for nothing in return

My Apa

That was my grandfather

# *Mother*

My Mother is the
Sun
Earth
Sky
Wind
Ocean
Flowers
Plants
My Mother is
Home
Strength
Power
Inspiration
Mi Mamá es Sol...es todo

# The One

You were the One

Before I knew I needed a One

Before I knew I deserved a One

I was the One

Before you knew you needed a One

Before you knew you wanted a One

We found the One in each other

And together we made One

The One

# Made with Love

It is of equal measure

My love and fear

I am both mesmerized and terrified by you

I am in awe and wonder of you

Where did you come from?

I know

From a place of pure joy and love

That's right

You came from my dreams

You were created before you were born

Made with love, infused with joy
and sprinkled with courage

A beautiful whirlwind

# The World Through Your Eyes

My favorite thing to do in the
world is watch you

Not just watch you

To observe

To admire

To witness

To see the world through your eyes

Through your wonderous spirit

What a joy it is to be your mother

What a blessing it is to call you my son

My son

# Because of You

Because of you I can navigate my own existence

Your eyes and ears in a world so different so
strange so scary and at times cruel

I'm sorry I didn't see it then, but I see it now

What a blessing to experience the
world from your perspective

A team of navigators, explorers

We saw it all

We heard it all

We felt it all

And together we conquered, together we are one

# Family

Once there were two
A family is born
Love, Sacrifice, Hard Work
Then there were three
Really the best time!
Love, Home, Foundation
Then came four
Growing Family
Siblings, Laughter, Play
Now there are five
We are complete
And through it all: Love
Familia, Together, Everlasting Bond
Forever My Family
J.S.P.S.H.

# Remembered

Everyone just wants to be found

To be found despite the noise despite the distractions despite the fast pace of the world

Do you see me? Do you hear me? Do I matter? Do your eyes sparkle when they meet mine?

Everyone just wants to be found

But to be remembered

That is the true desire

Now that you've found me, will you remember me?

# Final Thoughts

The story does not end here.

There is much more to write, much more to share.

There always is.

As long as you keep your eyes open,

Your ears attuned,

Your heart free,

All you have to do is ready the way... for
what's to come: healing blessings.


For they may come in the most unexpected
places, time and people.

"Where are you going?"
"To the Fireworks"...

# Reflection Pages
## for Your Own Journey

The final reflections are yours. These pages are here to capture your own thoughts, ideas and feelings. Here you can reflect on your own journey, whether you are beginning, continuing, or near the end.

........................................................................................................................................

........................................................................................................................................

........................................................................................................................................

........................................................................................................................................

........................................................................................................................................

........................................................................................................................................

........................................................................................................................................

........................................................................................................................................

........................................................................................................................................

........................................................................................................................................

........................................................................................................................................

........................................................................................................................................

........................................................................................................................................

........................................................................................................................................

........................................................................................................................................

........................................................................................................................................

........................................................................................................................................

........................................................................................................................................

........................................................................................................................................

........................................................................................................................................

........................................................................................................................................

........................................................................................................................................

........................................................................................................................................

........................................................................................................................................

........................................................................................................................................

........................................................................................................................................

........................................................................................................................................

........................................................................................................................................

........................................................................................................................................

........................................................................................................................................

........................................................................................................................................

........................................................................................................................................

........................................................................................................................................

# Acknowledgments

To all the people and places that have inspired me throughout my life: there will never be enough words or time to fully express the gratitude I feel for you. You have encouraged and sustained me.

Your boundless love has been my greatest source of strength, support and inspiration. It is the reason I find courage to move forward in the world even when it's scary, even when it's painful, even when others haven't believed in me.

You saw things in me that I didn't or couldn't see in myself. My writing is only a byproduct of my upbringing, mi cultura, mi fe, mi gente, and it is a reflection of the beauty you help me to see in the world.

Mom and Dad, this book does not get written without you. You didn't know it then, but your enthusiasm and investment in my curiosity and dreams have become the backbone on which I can do what I love best: move joy forward.

Special thank you to Kat Farley. Your beautiful artwork made this book come alive. I am forever grateful for you and your support on this journey. You are amazing.

**Self-Publishing**
School

## NOW IT'S YOUR TURN

**Discover the EXACT 3-step blueprint you need to become a bestselling author in as little as 3 months.**

Self-Publishing School helped me,
and now I want them to help
you with this FREE resource to begin outlining your book!

Even if you're busy, bad at writing, or
don't know where to start,
you CAN write a bestseller and build your best life.

With tools and experience across a
variety of niches and professions,
Self-Publishing School is the only resource you need to
take your book to the finish line!

### DON'T WAIT

Say "YES" to becoming a bestseller:

https://self-publishingschool.com/friend/

Follow the steps on the page to get a FREE resource
to get started on your book and unlock a discount
to get started with Self-Publishing School

# About The Author

**P**atricia Marquez-Singh **is the founder of Forward Joy Consulting, where she offers an integrated form of healing. Connecting spirituality and joy to social justice and equity is the basis of her life's work.**

Throughout her career, Patricia has created workshops on trauma responsive care, restorative practices, restorative justice, violence prevention and healing. As a certified Circle Keeper, she strives to lay the groundwork for collective healing to take place within organizations.

Patricia was born and raised in Hollister, California, and is very proud of her San Benito County roots. She now lives in Morgan Hill, California, with her husband and her baby boy James.

# Let's stay connected!

Thank you for reading my book!

I really appreciate all of your feedback, and
I love hearing what you have to say.

Please leave me an honest review on Amazon
letting me know what you thought of the book.

To receive bonus poems that didn't make
it into this book, send me an email.

Thank you from the bottom of my heart!

Patricia Marquez-Singh
forwardjoyps@gmail.com

Made in the USA
Middletown, DE
20 November 2024

65122486R00082